My Unfailing Love

Poems from Above

MY UNFAILING LOVE
Poems from Above

Sandra Burton Ord

Claritas Spiritual Theology®

Published 2023 by
Claritas Spiritual Theology®
London
claritas-st.com

No part of this publication may be reproduced, stored in a retrieval system or transmitted in any form or by any means, electronic, mechanical, photocopying, recording or otherwise, without the written permission of the publisher.

© 2023 Claritas Spiritual Theology

All rights reserved.

ISBN: 978-1-8384876-3-8

Cover & interior art by Sandra Burton Ord
Design by Denise Clare Oliver

To my loving daughters

Rebecca Jane & Sarah Louise

CONTENTS

INTRODUCTION 1
PRAYER TO THE HOLY SPIRIT 3
FIELD OF GRACE.. 5
HUSHED ARE YOU HEAVENLY NIGHT 7
THE WEEPING TREE 9
FRAGRANCE OF GRACE & LIGHT 11
THE GRACE OF JOY 13
HAVA – BREATH 15
SPIRITUAL COMMUNION ROSE................... 17
THE LENTEN MASS.. 19
THRESHOLD OF STILLNESS 21
SOUL BIRD'S SONG.. 23
ESSENCE OF UNKNOWING........................... 25
THE EDGE OF DARK... 27
I WAS IN PRISON & HE VISITED ME.......... 29
LOVE & SUFFERING 31
THE SEA GLASS PATH...................................... 33
SHÂBACH... 35

Introduction

Dear Readers,

As someone always more accustomed to painting, I was at first hesitant when I began to write. As I pondered on what was given without myself planning anything specific, the words, the inspirations seemed to become as pictures for me, so I could see what could be written.

While pondering more as to why this might be, I remembered my Great, Great, Great, Aunt, Mary Hutchinson who became wife of the poet William Wordsworth, and the hours of her dedication, carefully making copy of his poems.

In our old family volume, dated 1870, of Wordsworth poems, I found words which helped me enormously to have courage to put pencil to paper.

The works speaking of God being our home, in his ODE, *Imitations of Immortality from Recollections of early childhood:*

> Our birth is but a sleep and a forgetting:
> The soul that rises with us, our life's star,
> Hath had elsewhere its setting,
> And cometh from afar;
> Not in entire forgetfulness,
> And not in utter nakedness,
> But trailing clouds of glory do we come
> From God, who is our home.

These words opened for me a door to write, to welcome and greet others, and in my turn, to ponder on where we all belong.

Sandra Burton Ord.

Prayer to the Holy Spirit

Lord, you are the fire of my love,
The flame of my heart,
The burning purification of my soul.
You are the light of my day,
The reassurance of my darkness.

The heart of my desire is to serve you
with an everlasting flame of love
that leaps from my heart.

Oh sweet hearth of love divine,
Let me know the warmth
of Your perfect love received,
as in my home eternal I dare to hope.
Amen.

FIELD OF GRACE

This field of Grace is here for you,
Of living Hosts that feed all through
Your life of Blessings,
knowing this be true.

Every heart and soul, they'll ever renew.
Where else is found such nourishment,
but from the gift of Christ's own self?

Come gather all of what is here.
It heals, it soothes, it feeds, wipes tears.
Makes clear its purpose is for all
to love and cherish every human soul.

It is born of God's own very Grace,
With Spirit Blessed defines each day
and guides us forth all and every way,
that God has taught we ought be fed.

These flowering Hosts, forever fresh
await your reaping all they are worth.
Come gather now, this feast with all.

Your name is on your flower tall.
Accept your Holy Host with joy
And thankfulness all rich in faith.

It guides us forth on our daily way
with prayers, forgiveness if indeed we stray.
Never wander far from this Holy Place
Make home for you, The field of Grace.

Hushed are you heavenly night

Hushed are you heavenly night.
All earth awaits, as yet unknown,
the glory you will unveil.
Wrapped in secret, in deepest blue,
only The Star a sign of what is due.
As hushed are you heavenly night.

Until a burst of light appears
that fills the heavens with angelic choir.
Then shepherds kneel in wonder and awe
At what is told of Who is there,
Wrapped and swathed in a mother's care,
As hushed are you heavenly night.

Unknown to them, yet heaven inspired,
will follow those who've journeyed far,
wise enough to follow the Star,
and present such gifts of prophecy fare
As hushed are you heavenly night.

And now we too, this Holy Night, will

celebrate your coming Christ,
as still and silent, does earth yet know
the greatest secret you bestow?
As hushed are you heavenly night.

Yet stars escort you in Joseph's care,
while angel heralds adore in prayer,
and gentle mother takes up your hand,
and reassures God's only Son,
He's held in love, as love surrounds,
As hushed are you most heavenly night.

Majestic Grace and Prince of Peace,
we bring ourselves to your Birthday Feast.
We bring our love, our joy, our prayers,
in wonder, hushed as this Holy Night.

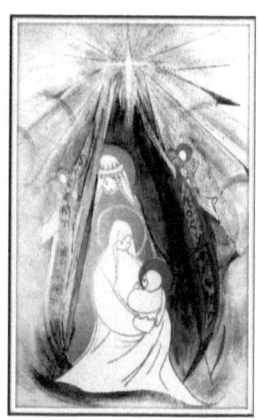

The Weeping Tree

I stood there waiting.
I stood there waiting,
cut down in my prime of life, my beauty gone.
I stood there waiting in man-made form,
forced to take another's life.
I stood there waiting. Waiting for whom?

+

HE came, and for a while, in pierced embrace,
I held ALL TRUTH, ALL LOVE, ALL GRACE.
The substance flowing down
my grain like balsam, was a mercy rain.
A stream of fragrant, healing love gushed out,
THE ESSENCE EGALITAIRE,
THE FORGIVENESS INFINITE.

+

Bathed in this Divinity, my earthly frame
would deeply bow in grief and in humility,
had I not had to wait of HE.

+

We waited.
We waited until THE HOUR.
We wait eternity, with love for you,
YOUR CHRIST and I, THE WEEPING TREE.

Fragrance of Grace & Light

From within its stillness the soul looked out,
watching and waiting, alert.
Daring to believe with joy,
the stirrings within itself
spoke truly of the coming one.
Then, from heaven afar,
it came in view with speed unknown.
Travelling within its own stillness,
It sought only, in believing stillness,
to be received.

The waiting soul saw nothing of its form or shape.
Nor wondered. It knew enough.
It was of the Spirit blessed, the Holy One of God.
Only when pierced,
did the soul know itself infused
with the holy fragrance.
A gift of grace and enlightenment.

Only then was the soul aware
of its own illumined self,

seeing and tasting the nourishing,
healing fruits it consumed,
as it was itself consumed,
in grace of sparkling radiance,
of purity crystal clear.

Sharp, and cutting deeply
into the consciousness of the soul,
it awakened the heart,
encouraged, to note for time eternal,
what had come to pass.
To pass thus from soul to soul,
now until eternity.

To awaken others to its call,
is the essence of its beckoning.
A yearning, seeking Creator of creation,
calling all home in grace and light,
to the eternal presence of Presence Eternal.

All earth itself observes,
as Fragrance follows the Spirit's will,
that seeks for souls of convert hearts,
who dare to trust and hope,
who watch and wait, alert.

The Grace of Joy

Grace of joy beheld, unheld,
Mysteriously three, yet only One.
Triune God of Creativity.

Grace of joy, in stillness blest,
Our hearts receive our souls requests
To hear the voice of God proclaim us
heirs to His kingdom and domain.

In celebration of gift of grace,
of gift of joy of time and space,
so deep within our mysterious place, indwelling,
hidden, is our God of Peace.

Grace of joy, so secret, so sublime,
for you and I,
yet known to all who search and seek,
and discover deep within themselves
the wonder of the grace of joy.

Then welcome there, the great mysterious Three,
The One Most Holy, THE BLESSED TRINITY.

Hava – breath

We are life, given and taken, yet still we are.
We await in hope, with faith,
the charity of thought.

The thought of us from you,
transformed to prayer
that calls for breath of Holy Spirit blessed,
to breathe on us anew
Grace of Life in God again.

Then from peace eternal our thanks will be,
Our prayers for you, from where we are.
Amen.

Spiritual Communion Rose

I call in need, Communion Rose,
Come fill my soul
with blessing of your presence.
Grace my heart with your healing love,
and fill until overflowing with joy,
knowledge that I am one with you.

One in fragrance, of Spiritual Communion,
blessed are we,
that neither time nor space
can separate or part.
Mystic, sweet, unseen, unheard,
from heaven your life in blossom guise
as fragile, fraternal, eternal bloom,
doth draw my being towards all my
soul knows wise.

Arise my being, my soul,
with Holy Spirit, in celebration.
With God's beloved and mine,
give thanks for grace bestowed and shared.

Sacrifice unique.
The Father's gift of His only Son,
Now as flowering eternal bloom, Spiritual Communion Rose, thou art mine.

The Lenten Mass

The presence of His forgiveness
gave me a moment's innocence
Taken out of my worldly place and being,
and lifted up in the arms
receiving the gift of my humble penitence
of then and now and when.
One moment raised, one moment offered,
the Body and Blood of Holy Innocence
shed for all, enveloping all.

Enveloping me,
enveloping my penitence and sorrow,
Borning it anew,
and drawing forth a soul
so cleansed with love
it knew the moment's innocence
of being embraced by our heavenly Father.
Being given the gift of a mantle
of inspiration to proclaim His name.

Lined with forgiveness,
a reminder of His warmth,
He knows I must return to praise His name

and offer again and again my frailty.

Without Him, innocence I cannot gain,
a need I have for returning home at last,
to live with Him.
Thus is the Holy Mass,
the gate of heaven,
forever open in our worldly place of being.

Threshold of Stillness

Goodness rested with me,
on the threshold of stillness,
of time filled with the presence of God's grace.
Truth wrote itself, I thought,
and wondered why my pen it's with?
My pen perhaps,
but God's own word was written.

Prayer had taught soul to listen,
To hear echoes in the silence.
It listened, then sang in praise,
thrice gladly, of goodness, truth and grace.

Hushed then, was soul at rest.
At peace, in goodness,
truth and grace embraced.
His coming was never heard,
for blessing entered first,
my soul to wake.
To converse known to both alone,
before His steps left again unheard,

but blessings stayed with blessings first,
as goodness, truth and grace remained.

Then, in the silence of stillness, another echo.
Soul's voice, in whispers deeply hushed,
was heard to say,
"Lord, I'm glad you came. Please come again."

Soul bird's song

The Lord has taught this little bird to sing.
To sing the praise, the shâbach of His glory.
This little soul-bird strains
against the confines of earth
and reaches in answer
to the beckoning of the unsearchable one.
Unsearchable by earthly means,
but lifted up on wings of prayer,
to the seen unseen,
and the finding of the unsearchable one.

Little soul-bird sings its desire
to reach beyond the friendship
of the one we know loves us,
and touch that light
which is no longer friendship without wings,
but love offered to love.

Little soul-bird believes it can soar to love,
not through grandness of spiritual marriage,
but like a child swept up into its father's arms.

The world may try and snatch and draw down,
pining with the need of patience, of humility,
but little soul-bird has need of flight.

The Spirit's breath comes by,
and scoops up little bird,
with song and pen and all.
The pruning trims to weightlessness
and lighted soul
is borne upon the breath of God
and hears his whispers in his transforming light.

A gust of wind upon the soul,
lifted like leaf upon the breeze,
soul-bird knows it will again descend,
its mortal state respect and serve,
but soul-bird's heart knows love lifts high,
its joy to share,
even if only in brief moments,
there is time allowed to spare,
for such love is always there.

Essence of Unknowing

Sated Spirit that breathes
breath of God upon the soul,
enveloping in darkness of unknowing,
truth in faith.

Thus Love has come to the soul in darkness,
and in this darkness it reaches out with touch,
The Essence of Love,
Him of whom the soul is taught
is Holy Word in Holy Church.

Within this Essence,
the soul new wisdom finds,
that is itself the very light
of darkness in souls unknowing.

The edge of dark

A prayer begun at early dawn
to blossom pure, with sorrow torn.
Remembrance of timeless love,
of Christ, The Lamb of God above.

Throughout the day, blessed Sacrifice,
our guide and friend, Redeemer be,
a flame of love to set us free
from all that troubles Christ and we.

As darkness comes, surrounds this grace,
its blossom never hides its face,
but weeps the more its tears of blood
to heal and bless as it only could.

Thus at the edge of dark, no fear should fall,
for Christ and guardian angel draw
great wings of light, of love of God
to stay the shadow's icy claw,
until the break of dawn once more.

I WAS IN PRISON & HE VISITED ME

Why does He carry me?
Is it because the world cannot see
That inner man that's really me?
Why am I here instead of thee?
Is it circumstances
that I have met, instead of thee?

+

Was it pain or hurt that drove me thus?
Was it fear or greed, revenge or hate?
Am I the rebel the world needs to hate?
Am I the innocent, a truth yet unveiled?
Is this man here the all of me?
Then why would He choose to carry me?

+

What does He see worthy
of a burden such as me?
To carry thus and walk with me?
Yet here He is in this small cell
to show me much the world won't see.
Does He invite me when once free,

to walk along that beach with He?
And if He says, "Come follow me",
will there be then, for the world to see
the footprints of a friend of He?

+++

Love & Suffering

When you suffer it is a secondary offering to Me.
The first and most important offering to Me
is your love.
Without love, what can be achieved
is not achieved.

+

A grace follows your yes.
Once you have said yes,
whatever I ask,
you can achieve,
because you belong to Me
in all ways, all paths, all being.
With this love comes trust.
Love, creates trust in suffering,
and makes all I ask, achievable in ways
you could before not comprehend.

+

Abandonment to Me
is the way GRACE is able to be.
Unite your mind
with your FATHER IN HEAVEN.
Unite your body with My SON'S suffering.

Unite your soul with My HOLY SPIRIT. BLESSINGS, from GOD THE FATHER.

The sea glass path

Soul, Soul, hold aloft the lantern of your heart,
and let it shed its light upon the path to me.
Here I await, in the centre of your soul,
as a beacon's fire of guardianship.

See before you again the path of colours,
bright and deep and gentle,
for they are broken moments,
days and years, I have gathered.

And, in my deepest deeps,
I have washed, soothed,
and healed into new life,
all the sorrows you have borne.

I have brought them home to you,
where they belong,
for Soul, Soul, thou art all mine,
and mine are now the jewels upon which you walk.

Soul, Soul, peer far within, and see,
with faith, your soul illumined.

There, in the indwelling light of colours
bright and deep, of sea-glass hues,
a path of truth and grace you'll find,
where old shoes of love I gave,
will now a consolation be,
and unite each step of yours with mine.

Shâbach

I praise and glorify your name my God,
and keep within my heart your stillness,
born of love, to soothe, and reconcile
with joy, the triumph of your saving love,
as into your hands, I commend my spirit.
Amen.

www.ingramcontent.com/pod-product-compliance
Lightning Source LLC
Chambersburg PA
CBHW030104100526
44591CB00008B/268